⚙ FUTURE ⚙
FILMMAKER

THIS BOOK BELONGS TO:

_____

⊗ **FUTURE FILMMAKER** ⊗

⊗ **FUTURE FILMMAKER** ⊗

⊗ **FUTURE FILMMAKER** ⊗

⊛ **FUTURE FILMMAKER** ⊛

⊛ **FUTURE FILMMAKER** ⊛

Printed in Great Britain
by Amazon